BASEBALL FROM THE BROADCAST BOOTH

So You Think You Know Baseball?

LEE ANDERSON

WESTBOW
PRESS®
A DIVISION OF THOMAS NELSON
& ZONDERVAN

Copyright © 2023 Lee Anderson.

All rights reserved. No part of this book may be used or reproduced by any means, graphic, electronic, or mechanical, including photocopying, recording, taping or by any information storage retrieval system without the written permission of the author except in the case of brief quotations embodied in critical articles and reviews.

WestBow Press books may be ordered through booksellers or by contacting:

WestBow Press
A Division of Thomas Nelson & Zondervan
1663 Liberty Drive
Bloomington, IN 47403
www.westbowpress.com
844-714-3454

Because of the dynamic nature of the Internet, any web addresses or links contained in this book may have changed since publication and may no longer be valid. The views expressed in this work are solely those of the author and do not necessarily reflect the views of the publisher, and the publisher hereby disclaims any responsibility for them.

Any people depicted in stock imagery provided by Getty Images are models, and such images are being used for illustrative purposes only.
Certain stock imagery © Getty Images.

ISBN: 978-1-6642-9557-5 (sc)
ISBN: 978-1-6642-9558-2 (hc)
ISBN: 978-1-6642-9556-8 (e)

Library of Congress Control Number: 2023905100

Print information available on the last page.

WestBow Press rev. date: 04/06/2023

Dedication

This book is dedicated to all the broadcasters who bring the game of baseball to life through their unique giftedness of calling a game.

Recognition

Thanks to Gordon Rumble for doing the drawings for this book. You're a good friend.
I want to give a special thank you to my wife, Sandy. Without her help this book would have been impossible. We have a lot of fun together and share the love of baseball.

_____
_____

_____

_____

_____

_____

_____

_____

_____

_____

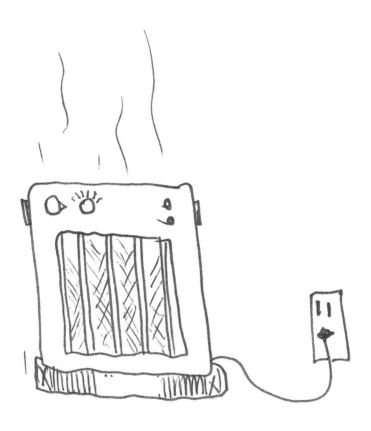

_____

_____

_____

_____

_____
_____

_____

_____

_____

_____

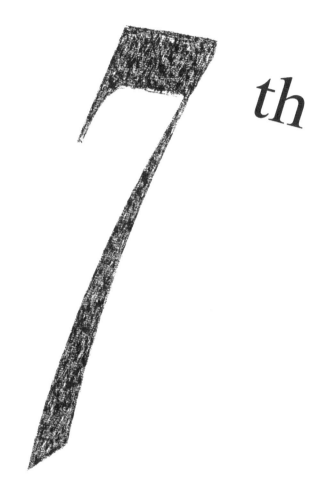

_____
_____

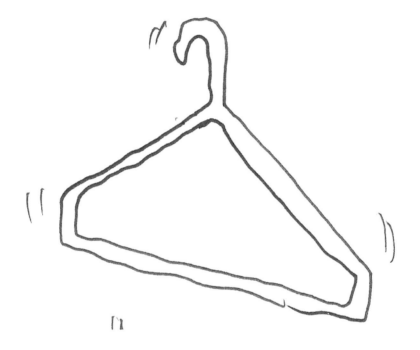

_____

_____

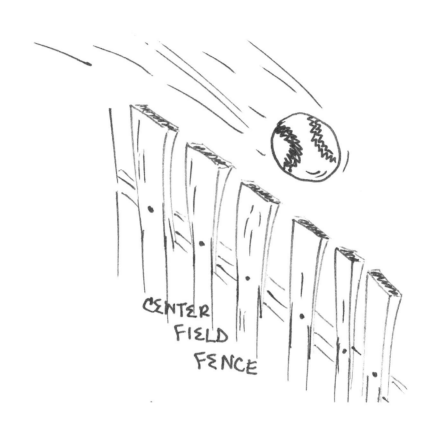

_____

_____

_____
_____

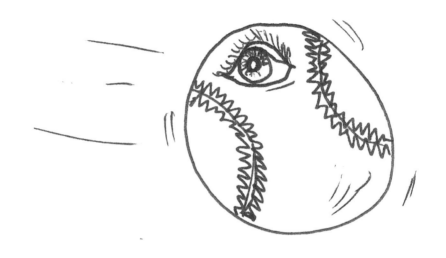

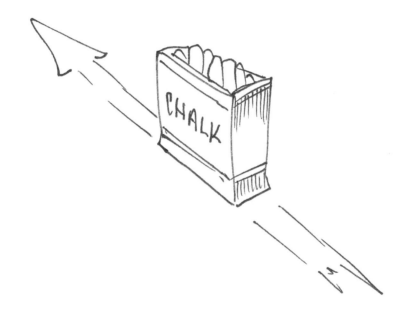

_____

_____

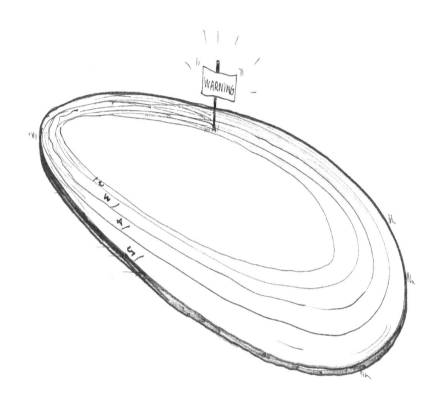

_____

_____

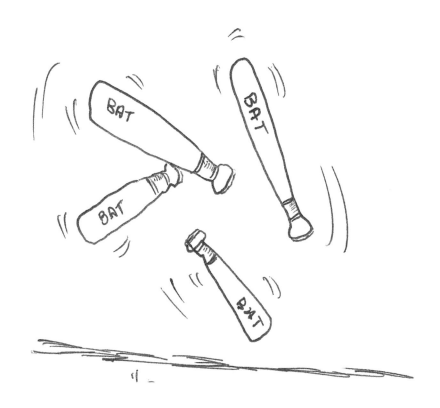

_____

_____

_____

_____

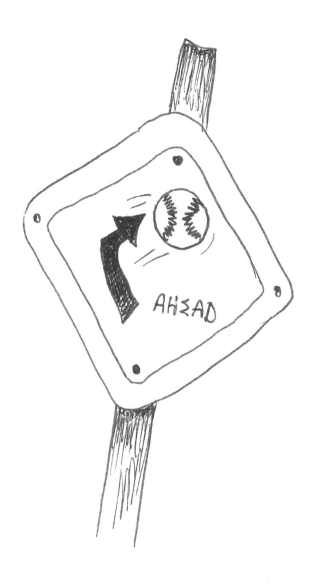

_____

_____

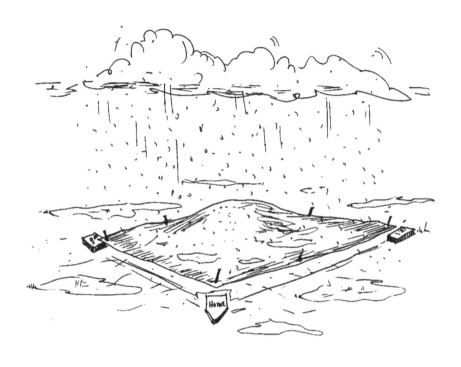

_____
_____

_____
_____

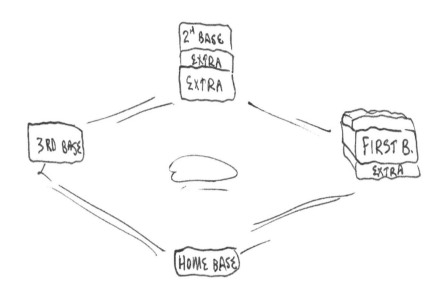

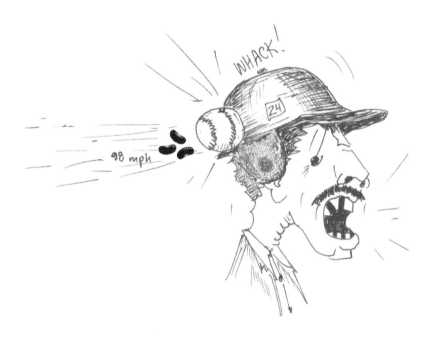

_____

_____

_____
_____

_____
_____

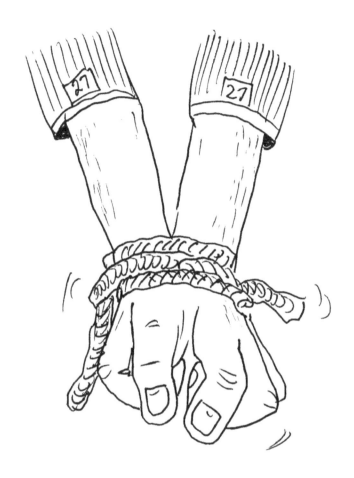

_____
_____

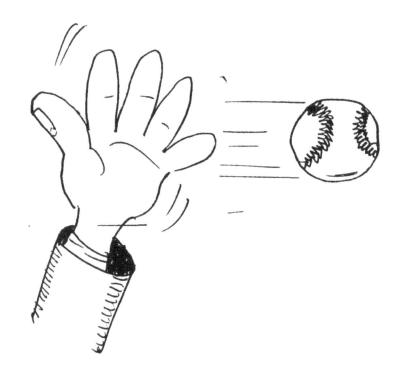

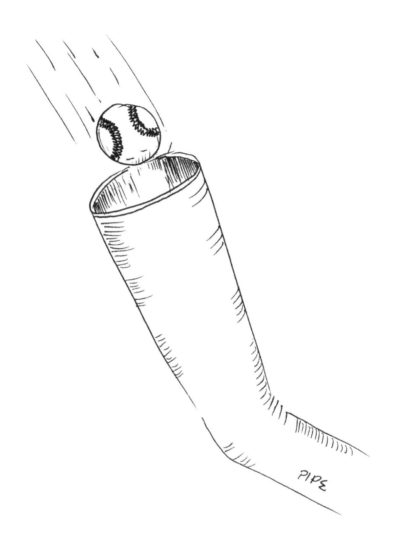

_____
_____

_____

_____

$$\begin{array}{r}6\\4\\3\\\hline=2\end{array}$$

BASEBALL ANSWERS

1. Barked at the Ump: Players hollering at the umpire.
2. Hit it a ton: Batter hit the ball hard.
3. Three bags: Batter hit the ball for three bases, also known as a triple.
4. Half swing: Batter did not swing through.
5. Triple play: Defensive team made three outs in one play.
6. The "Hill": The hill where the pitcher stands.
7. Pitcher taking the hill: Pitcher steps up on the hill to pitch.
8. Man behind the dish: Refers to the Umpire at home plate.
9. The "Plate": Refers to home plate.
10. Wake-up call: Batter hits the ball so hard toward a player that he doesn't have time to react.
11. Out of gas: Pitcher has lost his energy.
12. Long lead: Runner on base is getting several feet off the base.
13. Can of corn: Soft fly ball to the outfield.
14. Hit it on the nose: Bat hit the ball dead center.
15. Crack of the bat: Sound when the ball is hit perfectly.
16. Break in the action: Time-out has been called.
17. Ducks on the pond: More than one runner on base.
18. Spank the ball: Batter hit the ball hard.
19. Just got under it: Batter hit the ball below center of the ball.
20. Pulled the ball: Left handed batter hits the ball to the extreme right and a right handed batter hits the ball to the extreme left.
21. Pop-Up: Batter hits the ball high in the air and it is caught for an out.
22. Heater: Pitcher throws the ball really fast.
23. Head first slide: Base runner slides into the base head first.
24. Fork-ball: Special pitch that sinks at the last moment.
25. Throw to the plate: Player throws ball to home plate.
26. Toe the rubber: Pitcher put his foot on the pitching rubber.
27. Into the gap: Ball hit between two players.
28. Pulled the string: Pitcher strikes out the batter with a surprise pitch.

29. Poured it in there: Pitcher pitched the ball extremely hard.
30. Opener: Manager assigns a bull pin pitcher to start the game.
31. Barking up the wrong tree: Umpire blaming the wrong person for a verbal offence.
32. Action on the ball: Pitchers ball moves while in flight.
33. All arms and legs: Skinny pitcher has a lot of movement in his delivery.
34. Broke sharply: Pitched ball makes an unexpected movement.
35. Nailed him: Batter is hit by a pitch.
36. Ball was smoked: Ball hit very hard.
37. Ball was hammered: Ball hit very hard.
38. Pine Tar: Substance batter rubs on the handle of the bat for better grip.
39. Infield fly: Less than two out, runners on at least two bases, ball is hit high in the infield and the batter is immediately called out.
40. Base on balls: Batter goes to first base after pitcher fails to get him out.
41. 7th inning stretch: Break in the action and the crowd usually sings, "Take Me Out to the Ballgame"!
42. Spark-plug: A player who fires up the team!
43. Man stealing signs: Someone on the opposing team is trying to figure what sign(s) the other team is using for specific pitches or specific plays.
44. Ball sailed on him: Ball got away from the pitcher and flew out of reach of the catcher.
45. Save: Save is credited to a bull-pen pitcher in which his team is winning by 3 or fewer runs and finishes the game without losing the lead.
46. Hanger: A pitch that just floats into the strike zone.
47. Cutter: A pitch thrown that curves in the opposite direction.
48. Charge the mound: Usually a batter that gets hit by a pitch and goes after the pitcher in anger.
49. Digging in: Batter digs holes in the ground with his cleats to get better footing in the batter's box.
50. That ball is gone: Undeniable home run!
51. Breaking ball: Usually a curve ball that moves sideways.

52. Crushed the ball: Batter hits the ball hard.
53. Donut: A round weight placed on the bat to practice swing.
54. Eye on the ball: Batter keeps his eye on the ball.
55. Chalk line: Boundaries for batter's box, coaching box and foul lines outlines in chalk or white paint.
56. Bull pen: Location of the relief pitches during the game.
57. The "Mound": The pitching mound.
58. Paint the corner: Pitcher throws the ball that just goes over the edge of home plate.
59. Bunt: Batter doesn't swing but squares off to push the ball to keep it in the infield.
60. Down to the last out: Final out of the game.
61. Warning track: Area in the outfield just after the grass that is dirt before the fence.
62. Strike out: Forward K is a swinging strike out; backward K batter did not swing.
63. Bat flip: Batter flips his bat after hitting the ball.
64. Five tool player: A ball player exceptional in hitting, hitting with power, strong arm, speed, and fielding.
65. He yanked it!: The batter hit the ball extremely right or extremely left depending on if he is a right handed batter or left handed batter.
66. Dodged a bullet: Picher got out of the inning without losing the lead.
67. Bench cleared: When all players rush onto the field, usually a fight is ready to happen.
68. Autographed ball: When a player signs a ball for a fan.
69. Trapped the ball: It appears that the player caught the ball cleanly but it actually bounced on the ground first.
70. Bench coach: Manager's right hand coach.
71. Call to the bull pen: Manager makes a call to the bull pen for a new pitcher.
72. He will turn and watch it fly: When a fielder just knows that it is a home run.
73. Touched all four: The batter hit a home run and must touch all four bases.
74. Foul pole: Pole indicating out of bounds.

75. Short porch: Second deck in the outfield that is closer to home plate than the lower deck.
76. Curve: A pitch that starts straight and curves at the last moment.
77. Timely hitting: Usually when a batter drives in a run or runners on base.
78. Batter's box: The marked box where the batter stands while batting.
79. The Line-Up: Player's listed by batting order.
80. Meeting on the mound: When the coach, manager and players meet on the pitching mound to talk strategy to the pitcher.
81. Lit up the pitcher: Several batters have gotten hits during one inning.
82. Foul ball into the net: Foul ball hit into the netting behind home plate.
83. Merry-go-round: Bases loaded, two outs, 3 balls & 2 strikes on the batter, runners getting ready to move on pitchers first movement.
84. Snow cone: Fielder barely catches the ball in the tip of his glove.
85. Rain-out: Game is called because of rain. Unsafe for players to play.
86. Double-header: Two games played back to back in one day.
87. Cover the bases: Defensive player prepares to receive the ball and tag the base before the runner gets there.
88. Knuckle ball: Pitch thrown using primarily the knuckles.
89. Spit ball: A ball that is thought to have a foreign substance on it.
90. Extra bases: The batter hits a ball hard enough to get to second base or third base.
91. Bean ball: Batter gets hit in the helmet.
92. Stolen base: Runner successfully advance to the next base without being thrown out.
93. Batter got jammed: Batter hits the ball on the handle portion of the bat.
94. Drove the ball into the ground: Batter hit the ball straight down in front of home plate.
95. Switch hitter: Player that hits right or left handed.
96. Short fuse: Umpire gets angry easily.
97. In the hole: Two meanings – Batter hits the ball in-between players or the player in the dugout waiting to get into the on-deck circle.
98. Lazy fly ball: Softly hit fly ball.

99. Back door slider: Pitched ball that is thrown to the outside of the plate but then curves back towards the batter.
100. A heavy hitter: A consistently strong batter.
101. Punch out: Umpire call the batter out on strikes.
102. All aboard, next stop, Pound Town: Homerun call from Broadcaster.
103. Chin Music: Pitch is thrown near batters head.
104. Good morning, good afternoon, good-night: Batter strikes out on three pitches.
105. Chirping at the Ump: Players showing verbal displeasure from the dugout because of a bad call by the Umpire.
106. Club House: Player's locker room.
107. Threw a bullet to the plate: Strong, accurate throw by a player to home plate.
108. Bye, bye baby or that baby's gone: Without a doubt a home run.
109. Tomahawked the ball: Batter hit the ball with an overhand swing.
110. Sacrifice fly: Long fly ball that is caught but advances a runner to the next base.
111. Giving signs: Manager or coach signaling player as to what to do.
112. That ball was smoked: Ball was hit extremely hard.
113. A tapper to the mound: Ball softly hit on the ground toward the pitcher.
114. Check out his wheels: A runner with a lot of speed.
115. Around the horn: Ball is thrown to each player on the infield.
116. Utility player: A player that can play multiple positions.
117. Tied him up: A batter whose swing did not catch up to the ball.
118. That ball had mustard on it: An extremely fast pitch.
119. Jammed on the brakes: Runner comes to a quick stop.
120. Five finger fast ball: A pitch thrown using all four fingers and the thumb.
121. Back to back to back: Three home runs in a row.
122. Down the pipe: Ball thrown right over the center of home plate.
123. "Groundscrew": The personnel that takes care of the field.
124. He ran into a wall: Outfielder running into the outfield wall.
125. Spiked: A runner who stepped on another player.
126. Right down Broadway: Long home run.
127. Rung him up: Umpire called the batter out.

128. Screw ball: Pitched ball that is thrown to the outside of the plate and then curves toward the inside of the plate.
129. Slider: Pitch with movement to the right or to the left.
130. He stung the ball: Hit the ball extremely hard.
131. He drilled him: Pitcher hit the batter with the pitch.
132. Pick off: Pitcher gets a runner out before the player gets back to the base.
133. Batter's eye: The backdrop in center field that is usually green in color so the ball can be seen better by the batter.
134. Squeeze play: Batter bunts the ball with a runner on third base trying to get home before being thrown out.
135. Sacrificial lamb: A batter deliberately making an out to advance a runner.
136. He threw everything but the kitchen sink: Pitcher threw all of the pitches in his arsenal.
137. Double-barrel action in the bullpen: Left and right handed pitchers warming up at the same time in the bullpen.
138. Rung his bell: Pitched ball hit the batter in the head causing him to see stars!
139. 6+4+3=2: Shortstop (6) throws to second base (4) who throws to first base (3) for a double play (2).

CPSIA information can be obtained
at www.ICGtesting.com
Printed in the USA
BVHW031125260423
663000BV00002B/292